EPHE

Travel Guide 2026

Discover the Secrets of Ephesus: From Ancient Streets to Modern Comforts

ELIAS CALLOWAY

Copyright © 2026 by Elias Calloway

All rights reserved.

No part of this publication may be reproduced, distributed, or transmitted in any form or by any means, electronic or mechanical, including photocopying, recording, or any information storage and retrieval system, without the prior written permission of the author/publisher.

Legal Disclaimer:

This guide is intended for informational and entertainment purposes only. While every effort has been made to ensure the accuracy of the information within this book, travel conditions, prices, schedules, and regulations are subject to change without notice. The author and publisher are not responsible for any personal injury, property damage, loss, or inconvenience sustained by the user as a result of using this information.

TABLE OF CONTENTS

INTRODUCTION.. **5**
   Why Visit Ephesus?...7
   A Brief History of Ephesus.....................................9
   Best Time to Visit Ephesus.................................. 11
Getting to Ephesus..**13**
   How to Get There (By Air, Train, Bus).................. 14
   Transportation Within Ephesus............................ 16
   Tips for First-Time Visitors................................... 18
Accommodation in Ephesus.........................**22**
   Luxury Hotels and Resorts................................... 24
   Budget-Friendly Accommodation...........................25
   Guesthouses and Boutique Hotels........................ 27
Top Attractions in Ephesus...........................**30**
   The Ancient City of Ephesus................................ 31
   The Temple of Artemis...33
   The Great Theatre... 34
   The Library of Celsus...36
Hidden Gems in Ephesus..............................**38**
   The Terrace Houses.. 39
   The Baths of Varius... 41
   The Sacred Way.. 42
   The Fountain of Polio...44
Outdoor Activities and Adventures...........**46**
   Hiking in the Ephesus Region...............................47

Exploring the Beaches near Ephesus......................49
Boat Tours Along the Aegean Coast.......................50
Cultural Experiences...53
Local Festivals and Events......................................54
Turkish Cuisine: What to Try in Ephesus................56
Traditional Crafts and Souvenirs.............................58
Dining and Nightlife..60
Best Restaurants in Ephesus................................. 61
Traditional Turkish Dining Experiences.................. 63
Bars and Nightclubs in the Region.......................... 65
Shopping in Ephesus..67
Souvenir Shopping: What to Buy.............................68
Local Markets and Bazaar Guide............................ 70
Where to Find Authentic Turkish Textiles and Ceramics..71
Day Trips from Ephesus...74
Pamukkale and the Thermal Pools.........................75
Şirince Village: A Taste of Traditional Turkey..........77
Selçuk: Exploring the Surrounding Area.................78
Travel Tips for Ephesus... 81
Language and Communication Tips....................... 82
Currency and Payment Methods............................ 84
Safety and Health Tips..85
Local Etiquette and Customs..................................86
Practical Information..88
Opening Hours of Major Attractions........................89
Entrance Fees.. 90
Useful Local Contact Information............................92
Conclusion.. 94

INTRODUCTION

Located in **modern-day Turkey, Ephesus** stands as one of the most iconic and well-preserved ancient cities in the world. A true gem of the **ancient Mediterranean world**, Ephesus is renowned for its awe-inspiring **archaeological wonders, cultural richness**, and **historical significance**. This UNESCO World Heritage site invites travelers to step back in time and explore a city that was once a bustling hub of commerce, religion, and intellectual achievement.

Ephesus is a place where **Greek**, **Roman**, and **Byzantine** influences converge, offering an unforgettable journey through history. Some of its most famous landmarks include the majestic **Library of Celsus**, a grand building that once housed over 12,000 scrolls; the imposing ruins of the **Temple of Artemis**, one of the Seven Wonders of the Ancient World; and the **Great Theatre**, an architectural marvel that could hold up to 25,000 spectators. These landmarks, along with many others, tell the story of a city that was at the heart of the ancient world, from its rise as a Greek colony to its later significance under Roman rule.

Not just a city of monumental structures, Ephesus also holds great spiritual and cultural significance. It was a major religious center, home to the cult of **Artemis**, and later, it played an important role in early **Christianity**. Today, visitors can walk through the ruins of **Ephesus**, where the remains of ancient temples, houses, and streets still evoke a profound sense of awe.

With its remarkable blend of history, culture, and architecture, **Ephesus** should be on every traveler's list. It is a place where ancient history comes alive, and every corner offers a new discovery waiting to be explored.

Why Visit Ephesus?

Ephesus is more than just an archaeological site—it's a portal into the past, where visitors can **explore** one of the most significant and well-preserved cities of the ancient world. The city's **historical, cultural,** and **archaeological value** is unmatched, offering an immersive experience that brings ancient history to life.

One of the main attractions in Ephesus is the **Temple of Artemis**, a **magnificent wonder** that once stood as one of the **Seven Wonders of the Ancient World**. Though only the foundations and a single column remain today, the temple's historical significance is undeniable. The **Library of Celsus**, another iconic monument, is a marvel of ancient architecture with its grand facade and once-extensive collection of manuscripts. It was not only a library but also a **mausoleum** for its benefactor, **Tiberius Celsus**.

The **Great Theatre** of Ephesus is also a must-see, a massive amphitheater capable of seating 25,000 spectators. It remains one of the most well-preserved theaters from the ancient world and is still used for performances today, offering visitors a sense of how the people of ancient Ephesus would have experienced entertainment.

Beyond these magnificent ruins, Ephesus offers a rich **cultural experience** as you walk through its ancient streets. The **Terrace Houses** showcase elegant frescoes and mosaics that provide a glimpse into the lives of the city's wealthier residents, while the **St. John Basilica** marks the spot where **the Apostle John** is believed to have been buried, tying the city's history to early Christianity.

Practical Tips:

- **Must-See Attractions**: Don't miss the **Library of Celsus**, the **Great Theatre**, and the **Terrace Houses**. The **Temple of Artemis** and **St. John Basilica** are also essential stops for history and religious significance.
- **Navigating the Site**: Ephesus is large, so **wear comfortable shoes** and be prepared for a lot of walking. A guide or audio guide can help bring the history alive as you explore the ruins.
- **Time to Visit**: Plan for at least **3-4 hours** to explore the city properly, or even a full day if you want to take your time and visit the surrounding sites.

Ephesus is a place where the past is not just preserved but experienced in a vivid and profound way, making it one of the most compelling destinations in the ancient world.

A Brief History of Ephesus

Ephesus' history stretches back over two millennia, evolving from a small Greek settlement to one of the greatest cities of the ancient Mediterranean. The city's origins date back to the **10th century BC**, when the Greeks established a colony near the **Cayster River**. Over time, it grew into a prosperous city, known for its stunning architecture, vibrant marketplace, and strategic location.

The **Temple of Artemis** was one of Ephesus' earliest and most significant landmarks, dedicated to the goddess Artemis and standing as a symbol of the city's religious and cultural importance. Ephesus was a thriving center of trade, attracting merchants and scholars from across the ancient world. Its harbor was a key maritime hub, facilitating commerce between the East and West.

In the **6th century BC**, the city was conquered by the Lydians, and then later, in the **4th century BC**, it came under the rule of the **Persians**. The Greeks returned after defeating the Persians, and Ephesus became part of the **Hellenistic world**. Under **Roman rule** in the 1st century BC, the city flourished, becoming one of the empire's most important cities. It was during this period that the **Library of Celsus** was constructed, and **Ephesus** reached its peak in terms of wealth and cultural significance.

Ephesus also holds great religious significance in the early days of **Christianity**. The **Apostle Paul** visited the city and preached to its citizens, and **St. John** is believed to have spent his later years here. Ephesus became an important early Christian center, and the **Basilica of St. John** was constructed in his honor.

However, by the **7th century AD**, Ephesus began to decline due to **shifting trade routes**, **earthquakes**, and the silting of its harbor. By the Middle Ages, much of the city was abandoned, leaving behind the **incredible ruins** that draw visitors to this day.

Historical Context: Ephesus' blend of Greek, Roman, and Christian heritage offers visitors a unique opportunity to experience the diverse cultural influences that shaped this ancient city. Understanding the city's religious, political, and commercial significance helps deepen the experience of exploring its ruins.

Best Time to Visit Ephesus

The best time to visit Ephesus is during the **spring (April to June)** and **fall (September to October)** months. These seasons provide **ideal weather** for exploring the ruins—**mild temperatures**, clear skies, and fewer crowds than the summer months, making it more comfortable to wander through the ancient streets and landmarks.

In the spring, temperatures typically range from **15°C to 25°C (59°F to 77°F)**, while in the fall, it's similar, offering a pleasant climate for sightseeing. Both seasons offer an excellent opportunity to avoid the **summer heat**, which can often exceed **35°C (95°F)**, making it challenging to explore the expansive archaeological site comfortably.

Practical Tips:

- **Summer Heat**: If you visit during the summer, be prepared for intense heat. It's advisable to start your day early, wear a **wide-brimmed hat**, and bring plenty of **water**. You may also want to wear lightweight, breathable clothing to stay comfortable.
- **Avoiding Crowds**: Spring and fall not only offer the best weather but also fewer tourists than the peak summer months. These shoulder seasons are the perfect time for those who prefer a more peaceful visit.
- **Cultural Events**: Ephesus is close to **Selçuk**, where you can experience local festivals, particularly during the **spring and summer** months. If you're interested in **local culture**,

check the event calendar for **festivals** like the **Ephesus Festival**, which celebrates local music, dance, and heritage.

To ensure the best experience, plan your visit during the cooler months to avoid the crowds and enjoy a more comfortable, leisurely exploration of the ancient city.

Getting to Ephesus

Ephesus is easily accessible from major cities in **Turkey**, with several convenient transportation options. The closest major airport is **İzmir Adnan Menderes Airport**, located about **50 kilometers (31 miles)** from **Ephesus**. Visitors can fly directly into İzmir from major Turkish cities like **Istanbul**, **Ankara**, and **Antalya**. The airport is well-connected with **direct flights** from Istanbul (about **1 hour** flight time), making it one of the most convenient gateways for travelers coming from abroad.

Once you arrive at **İzmir Adnan Menderes Airport**, there are several transportation options to get to **Ephesus**. The easiest and most affordable way is to take a **train** or **bus** to the nearby town of **Selçuk**, which is only a **15-minute drive** from the archaeological site. **Buses** to **Selçuk** depart regularly from the airport or **İzmir's city center** and typically take about **1 hour**. Alternatively, you can take a **train** from **İzmir's Basmane Station** to Selçuk (approximately **1.5 hours**), with trains running several times a day.

If you prefer a more direct option, **taxis** or **private transfers** are available at the airport, but these can be more expensive, typically costing between **€50-70** depending on traffic.

13

Practical Tips:

- **Flights**: Book your **flights** in advance for the best deals, especially during peak tourist seasons.
- **Transportation**: For budget-conscious travelers, **buses** or **trains** are the most economical way to get to Ephesus, while taxis offer convenience but at a higher cost.
- **Travel Time**: Plan for about **2 to 3 hours** of travel time from **İzmir Adnan Menderes Airport** to **Ephesus** via public transport.

How to Get There (By Air, Train, Bus)

Ephesus is located in **Selçuk**, a small town in the İzmir Province, and is best accessed via **İzmir Adnan Menderes Airport**. The airport is a major hub with direct flights from cities like **Istanbul** (about **1 hour**), **Ankara**, and **Antalya**. For international travelers, flights from **Istanbul** are frequent and offer the most convenient entry point to the region.

Once you arrive at **İzmir Adnan Menderes Airport**, there are several transportation options to reach **Selçuk**, the closest town to **Ephesus**:

- **Train**: From **İzmir's Basmane Station**, take a **train** to **Selçuk**. The journey takes about **1.5 hours**, and trains run multiple times a day, offering a comfortable and affordable option.
- **Bus**: There are also **buses** available from **İzmir** (including the airport) to **Selçuk**, taking about **1 hour**. Buses depart regularly from the **İzmir Otogar (main bus station)** and other transport hubs. This is an affordable way to travel to the archaeological site.
- **Taxi**: Taxis are available from **İzmir Adnan Menderes Airport** directly to **Selçuk** and take about **45 minutes**. While more expensive, taxis are a convenient option for those with heavy luggage or looking for a quicker journey.

Practical Tips:

- **Tickets**: **Train tickets** can be purchased at the station, while **bus tickets** are available at the airport or bus stations in **İzmir**.
- **Public Transport**: Trains and buses are reliable and affordable, though travelers should account for some wait times. Taxis are more direct but costly.

Transportation Within Ephesus

Once in **Ephesus**, getting around is straightforward, as the main archaeological site is **open-air** and walkable. **Walking** is the most common and enjoyable method of exploring the ruins. The site is large, so visitors will do a lot of walking, especially between key landmarks such as the **Library of Celsus**, **Great Theatre**, and **Temple of Artemis**. Be prepared to spend **2 to 3 hours** walking around the site to fully appreciate the ancient city's splendor.

For those looking for a bit more convenience, there are **shuttle buses** that run between the **site entrance** and key spots like the **Terrace Houses** or **Virgin Mary's House**, which is a bit further from the main site. These can be a good option if you're short on time or prefer not to walk too much.

Additionally, **taxis** are available from **Selçuk** to **Ephesus** for visitors who want to avoid walking or need a quick ride to the site or nearby attractions like the **Temple of Artemis** or **Virgin Mary's House**.

Practical Tips:

- **Walking**: Wear comfortable **shoes** and bring a **hat** and **sunscreen** for walking around the site. The sun can be intense, especially in summer.

- **Guided Tours**: Consider hiring a **guide** or using an **audio guide** to enhance your experience. Guided tours provide valuable historical context that makes the ruins come to life.

To get the most out of your visit, take your time to walk through the streets of ancient Ephesus, exploring the impressive ruins and learning about the city's fascinating past.

Tips for First-Time Visitors

Visiting **Ephesus** is a fantastic journey through time, but to make the most of your experience, there are a few practical tips every first-time visitor should know:

- **Weather Preparedness**: Ephesus experiences a **Mediterranean climate**, with hot summers and mild winters. If you're visiting in summer (June to August), be prepared for **high temperatures**, often exceeding **30°C (86°F)**. Be sure to wear **comfortable shoes**, a **wide-brimmed hat**, and bring **plenty of water** to stay hydrated while exploring the ancient ruins. The best times to visit are in **spring (April to June)** and **fall (September to October)**, when the weather is more temperate and the crowds are thinner.

- **What to Wear**: Since you'll be walking through **uneven terrain, comfortable walking shoes** are a must. **Light, breathable clothing** is ideal for hot weather, but bring a light jacket for cooler mornings or evenings. Don't forget **sunscreen** and **sunglasses**, as much of the site is exposed to the sun.
- **Ticketing**: You can **purchase tickets** to the archaeological site at the entrance or online. To avoid long lines, it's recommended to **buy tickets in advance** or arrive early, especially during peak tourist seasons. Consider getting a **combined ticket** if you plan to visit **Terrace Houses** or the **Ephesus Museum**.
- **Guided Tours**: While **self-guided tours** are great, hiring a **local guide** or using an **audio guide** will enrich your experience. A knowledgeable guide can provide fascinating insights into the history and significance of the site, bringing the ruins to life.
- **Nearby Attractions**: Ephesus is close to several other **must-see attractions**. Don't miss the **Temple of Artemis**, one of the **Seven Wonders of the Ancient World** (though only ruins remain), and the **Virgin Mary House**, where it's believed that **Mary** spent her final years. The **Ephesus Museum** in **Selçuk** offers artifacts from the ruins, providing further historical context.

- **Staying Hydrated**: The ancient site can be quite large, and temperatures can climb quickly. Be sure to **stay hydrated**, especially if visiting during the warmer months. **Water fountains** are available throughout the site, but bringing a refillable **water bottle** is always a good idea.

By planning ahead and following these tips, you'll ensure a comfortable and enriching experience at **Ephesus**. From its monumental ruins to its profound history, this ancient city is a truly unforgettable destination.

Accommodation in Ephesus

When visiting **Ephesus**, the most convenient place to stay is in the nearby town of **Selçuk**, located just a short distance from the ancient site. Selçuk offers a wide range of accommodation options, from budget-friendly stays to luxurious resorts, catering to various preferences and budgets.

For those seeking **luxury**, Selçuk has upscale hotels with **modern amenities** like **pools**, **spas**, and **fine dining**, offering a peaceful retreat after a day of exploring the ruins. For **mid-range options**, there are plenty of comfortable **boutique hotels** and **guesthouses** that offer personalized service and a cozy atmosphere, often located within walking distance of the **Ephesus site**.

If you're traveling on a **budget**, Selçuk also offers several **affordable hotels**, **hostels**, and **guesthouses** that provide basic comforts like **free Wi-Fi** and **breakfast**. These options are perfect for travelers who want to keep costs low but still enjoy a comfortable stay near major attractions.

For travelers looking for a more **authentic experience**, staying in one of the family-run **guesthouses** in Selçuk or the surrounding villages is a great choice. These accommodations offer a chance to experience Turkish hospitality firsthand, with warm hosts providing local insights and homemade breakfasts.

Practical Tips:

- **Location**: Choose accommodations within walking distance of the **Ephesus ruins** for easy access.
- **Peak Season**: If visiting during peak season (spring and fall), be sure to **book in advance** to secure your preferred accommodation.
- **Transportation**: Most accommodations in **Selçuk** are well-connected by local buses or taxis, making it easy to reach **Ephesus** and nearby attractions.

No matter your budget, Selçuk provides a variety of lodging options that make it the perfect base for exploring Ephesus and the surrounding area.

Luxury Hotels and Resorts

For those seeking a **luxurious stay** near **Ephesus**, the **Selçuk** and **Kusadasi** regions offer several high-end hotels and resorts that combine elegance, comfort, and proximity to the ancient ruins. These properties not only provide world-class service but also allow guests to relax in style after exploring the remarkable archaeological site.

One standout property is the **Aqua Fantasy Aquapark Hotel & Resort**, located in **Kusadasi**, just a short drive from Ephesus. This luxury resort offers **ocean views**, a **private beach**, and a **huge waterpark**, perfect for families or those seeking a more relaxed experience after a day of sightseeing. Another popular option is the **Korumar Hotel**, which boasts **sea views**, **luxurious rooms**, and **fine dining**, offering an elegant experience for travelers looking to unwind in comfort.

For a more **historically rich experience**, consider staying in the **Suhan 360 Hotel** in **Kusadasi**, which features a mix of **modern luxury** and **traditional charm**, with a **spa, pool,** and **restaurant overlooking the Aegean Sea**.

Practical Tips:

- **Booking**: These luxury hotels fill up quickly, particularly in the **high season** (spring and summer). Be sure to **book in advance** to secure the best rates and availability.
- **Price Range**: Expect to pay around **€100-250 per night** for a luxury hotel, with higher rates for premium services like spa treatments and sea-view rooms.

- **Proximity**: All luxury hotels are well-connected to the **Ephesus archaeological site**, either by a short drive or private transport options.

For travelers who want a **refined and relaxing experience** while visiting one of the most significant historical sites in the world, these luxury hotels and resorts provide the ultimate comfort and convenience.

Budget-Friendly Accommodation

Ephesus is accessible to travelers on all budgets, and those seeking **affordable yet comfortable** accommodations will find plenty of options in **Selçuk**, the town closest to the ancient ruins. For budget-conscious visitors, **affordable hotels**, **hostels**, and **small guest houses** provide cozy stays with the basic amenities needed for a pleasant visit.

Hotel Bella in Selçuk is a popular budget option, offering **clean rooms**, **free Wi-Fi**, and **complimentary breakfast** for a reasonable price. Another great budget choice is the **Atilla's Getaway**, a **family-run guesthouse** that offers comfortable rooms with **traditional Turkish décor** and a welcoming atmosphere. For those traveling with a group or solo, **Selçuk Hostel** offers dormitory-style rooms with access to a **shared kitchen** and common spaces.

These affordable accommodations are located just a short walk or bus ride from the **Ephesus ruins**, making them convenient for visitors. They often provide guests with insider tips on local attractions, as well as **personalized recommendations** for nearby restaurants, markets, and cultural experiences.

Practical Tips:

- **Price Range**: Expect to pay around **€20-50 per night** for budget stays, depending on the season and room type.
- **Book Early**: To get the best rates and avoid last-minute price hikes, **book your accommodation in advance**, especially during peak tourist season.
- **Amenities**: Many budget accommodations offer free **Wi-Fi**, breakfast, and sometimes even **transportation** to local attractions.

With plenty of budget-friendly options in **Selçuk**, visiting Ephesus doesn't have to break the bank. Travelers can enjoy a comfortable stay while keeping their expenses low, allowing them to fully immerse themselves in the history and culture of this remarkable ancient city.

Guesthouses and Boutique Hotels

For travelers seeking a more **personalized** and **intimate** experience, **guesthouses** and **boutique hotels** around **Ephesus** offer a unique blend of comfort and **Turkish hospitality**. These accommodations provide a cozy, charming atmosphere that allows guests to truly immerse themselves in the local culture while enjoying a relaxing stay.

Many of these boutique properties are housed in **restored historic buildings**, adding an extra layer of charm to the experience. **Ephesus Boutique Hotel** in **Selçuk**, for example, is a beautiful guesthouse that combines **traditional Turkish design** with **modern comforts**, offering guests a peaceful retreat close to the ancient ruins. The **Aegean Dream Hotel** offers stylish rooms with traditional Turkish décor and is well-known for its warm hospitality, offering personalized service from the owners.

A standout feature of these **family-run guesthouses** is the opportunity to enjoy a homey atmosphere, often with homemade **Turkish breakfasts** and personal recommendations for **local experiences**. Staying at a guesthouse also provides the opportunity to meet other travelers in a relaxed and welcoming environment.

Practical Tips:

- **Price Range**: Expect to pay around **€30-70 per night** for guesthouses and boutique hotels, depending on the location and amenities.
- **Quiet Surroundings**: These accommodations offer a **quieter, more peaceful environment**, making them perfect for those looking to escape the crowds of the more commercialized hotels.
- **Proximity**: Most boutique hotels are located within easy reach of **Ephesus** and **Selçuk town center**, often within walking distance to the **Ephesus Archaeological Site**.

If you value **authenticity** and **personalized service**, staying at a **guesthouse** or **boutique hotel** in **Selçuk** offers a warm, intimate experience that combines comfort, style, and local charm. These accommodations provide an excellent way to enjoy the wonders of **Ephesus** while embracing the warmth and hospitality of Turkish culture.

Top Attractions in Ephesus

Ephesus, a captivating blend of **ancient history**, **culture**, and **religion**, offers visitors an unforgettable experience of the ancient world. Its **archaeological significance** lies in the integration of **Greek**, **Roman**, and early **Christian influences**, creating a fascinating historical tapestry that is visible in every ruin.

A must-see is the **Library of Celsus**, one of the most iconic and well-preserved structures in Ephesus. This monumental library, with its intricate **Corinthian columns** and **beautiful carvings**, once housed thousands of scrolls and served as a **tomb** for **Tiberius Julius Celsus**. Not far from the library is the **Great Theatre**, a massive amphitheater capable of holding up to **25,000 spectators**. It's famous for its remarkable **acoustics** and its connection to the **Apostle Paul**, who preached here in the early days of Christianity.

Further down the path lies the **Temple of Artemis**, one of the **Seven Wonders of the Ancient World**. While only a single column remains today, the scale of the temple once dwarfed many of the other monuments in the city. Its significance as a center of worship for the goddess Artemis underscores the **religious** and **cultural** importance of Ephesus in ancient times.

Other notable attractions include the **Terrace Houses**, where visitors can witness stunning **mosaics** and **frescoes** preserved over the centuries, and the **Stadium**, where ancient athletic events once took place.

Ephesus is a unique site where you can walk in the footsteps of ancient civilizations, feeling the weight of history at every corner.

The Ancient City of Ephesus

Once a thriving port city and a key metropolis in the **Roman Empire**, **Ephesus** is an archaeological wonder that offers an in-depth glimpse into ancient urban life. The city's **layout** showcases the ingenuity of its builders, with its **marble streets**, **public squares**, and **temples** all designed to serve both **cultural** and **commercial purposes**.

Ephesus' main artery is the **Curetes Street**, which runs from the **Theatre** to the **Temple of Artemis**, lined with **marble columns** and **ancient shops**. As you walk, you'll pass the **Roman bathhouses**, the **Agora**, and the **fountain of Trajan**, all illustrating the city's importance as a **trade hub** and **center of social life**.

The **Terrace Houses** offer a fascinating look into the **domestic life** of Ephesus, where the wealthy elite lived in multi-roomed homes adorned with stunning **mosaics** and **frescoes**. Nearby, the **Temple of Hadrian**, with its beautifully preserved arches, honors the emperor and demonstrates the city's architectural prowess.

At the southern end of the site is the **Great Theatre**, a testament to Ephesus' role as a center of **entertainment** and **culture**. It could hold up to **25,000 spectators**, used for theatrical performances and political gatherings.

Visiting Ephesus requires walking extensively, so **comfortable shoes** are a must. To fully explore the site, allocate at least **3-4 hours**, or longer if you want to delve deeper into the **Terrace Houses** or visit the **Ephesus Museum** in nearby Selçuk for further context.

The Temple of Artemis

Once standing as one of the **Seven Wonders of the Ancient World**, the **Temple of Artemis** in Ephesus was an extraordinary feat of architecture dedicated to the goddess Artemis, the protector of the city. This **grand sanctuary**, completed around **550 BCE**, was a monumental structure, standing approximately **115 meters** long and **55 meters** wide, far surpassing many other temples of its time. Its columns, which stood over 18 meters tall, were adorned with sculptures and offerings, making the temple not only a place of worship but also a symbol of the city's **wealth** and **spiritual importance**.

Today, only a single **column** remains from the temple, but it still provides a striking sense of the temple's original grandeur. Ancient historians like **Herodotus** and **Pliny the Elder** recorded its magnificence, further cementing its place in history.

Over time, the temple suffered multiple **destructions**—it was burned down in **356 BCE** by **Herostratus**, and later rebuilt by **Alexander the Great** and others. The ruins that remain today reflect the site's tumultuous history.

Practical Tips:

- **Visiting**: The Temple of Artemis is located just outside the main ruins of Ephesus. You can reach it by **walking** from the main site or by **taxi** from **Selçuk** (about **5 minutes**).
- **Nearby Attractions**: After visiting the temple's ruins, consider heading to the nearby **Ephesus Archaeological Museum** in Selçuk to view the temple's sculptures and **artifacts**.

The Temple of Artemis remains one of the most **legendary** monuments in the ancient world, offering a powerful reminder of the ancient worship practices and architectural mastery of its builders.

The Great Theatre

The **Great Theatre of Ephesus** is one of the most **impressive** and well-preserved structures in the city, showcasing the grandeur of Ephesus as a **cultural** and **entertainment** hub. Capable of seating around **25,000 spectators**, it was the largest theatre in the ancient world and could host a variety of events, from **dramatic performances** to **political gatherings**.

What makes the theatre especially remarkable is its **acoustics**. Even today, the sound quality is so precise that a person standing at the center of the stage can be heard clearly from every seat, demonstrating the advanced engineering of its creators. The **Greek-style theatre** was later expanded by the Romans and retains many of its original features, including the **scenic facade** and **orchestra** area where performers once stood.

In addition to its architectural beauty, the theatre holds **biblical significance**. It is said to be the place where **Apostle Paul** preached, and where he faced opposition from the city's silversmiths, who made idols of Artemis, sparking a riot.

Practical Tips:

- **Best Viewpoints**: The highest seating levels offer the best **panoramic views** of the surrounding ruins and Ephesus itself.
- **Best Time to Visit**: Early in the morning or late afternoon, when the sun isn't too harsh, provides the best **lighting** and fewer crowds.

The Great Theatre is one of the most **dramatic** and **immersive** sites in Ephesus, offering visitors a glimpse into the world of ancient performances and a fascinating connection to **biblical history**.

The Library of Celsus

The **Library of Celsus** is one of Ephesus' most iconic and **photographed** landmarks. Built around **135 CE** in honor of **Tiberius Julius Celsus**, the Roman senator and governor, the library was both a **tomb** and a **library**, housing over **12,000 scrolls**. Its stunning **facade** features **Corinthian columns**, intricate carvings, and statues of gods and goddesses, showcasing the advanced architecture of the Roman period.

Once a monumental building, the library's interior was destroyed in an earthquake, but the facade was reconstructed in the 1970s, offering visitors a chance to marvel at its grandeur. The **columns** are adorned with **marble reliefs**, while statues representing **Wisdom**, **Knowledge**, and **Virtue** line the facade.

The Library of Celsus was one of the most **important libraries** in the ancient world, second only to Alexandria's. It functioned as a **center of learning**, attracting scholars from around the Roman Empire.

Practical Tips:

- **Photography**: The **best time** for photography is early morning or late afternoon when the lighting enhances the architectural beauty of the facade.
- **Nearby Attractions**: The **Gate of Mazeus and Mithridates**, just next to the library, offers a great opportunity to see another part of the city's grandeur.

The Library of Celsus remains a **masterpiece** of Roman architecture, symbolizing the city's legacy as a cultural and intellectual hub.

Hidden Gems in Ephesus

While the grand attractions like the **Library of Celsus** and **Great Theatre** steal the spotlight, Ephesus is full of lesser-known treasures that provide a richer, more intimate exploration of the city's fascinating history. These **hidden gems** offer a glimpse into daily life, spirituality, and advanced engineering of the ancient world.

One such hidden gem is the **Terrace Houses**, also known as the "houses of the rich." Located on **Curetes Street**, these luxurious residences offer an extraordinary look at Roman domestic life, with **well-preserved frescoes**, intricate **mosaics**, and spacious rooms with **central courtyards**. The elaborate **frescoes** and **mosaics** depict scenes from mythology, daily life, and nature, showcasing the cultural sophistication of Ephesus's wealthy citizens.

Another overlooked site is the **Baths of Varius**, a Roman bath complex that served as both a public bathhouse and a social center. The intricate **hypocaust system** (underfloor heating) and **marble floors** offer a glimpse into Roman architectural prowess and their emphasis on cleanliness and socializing.

The **Sacred Way**, an ancient ceremonial road once used during religious festivals and processions, is another fascinating site. Lined with **marble columns**, **statue bases**, and remnants of sculptures, walking the path connects you to the city's **spiritual heart**—the **Temple of Artemis**.

Finally, the **Fountain of Polio**, an elegant water monument, stands as a testament to Roman engineering. Located near the **State Agora**, this structure provides water to the city, with **decorative reliefs** and **intricate stonework** showcasing Roman artistry and utility.

Practical Tips:

- These attractions require **separate tickets**, so be sure to **budget time** for these hidden gems.
- For a quieter experience, visit during **early morning** or **late afternoon**, avoiding peak hours.

The Terrace Houses

Located along **Curetes Street** in the ancient city of **Ephesus**, the **Terrace Houses** provide an extraordinary glimpse into the life of the city's elite during the Roman period. These well-preserved residences were the homes of **wealthy citizens**, showcasing a level of sophistication that would rival any modern-day mansion.

The homes are organized around **central courtyards** and are adorned with **vivid frescoes** and **intricate mosaics** that reveal the tastes and beliefs of the time. The **mosaics** depict scenes from **Greek mythology**, while the **frescoes** feature intricate designs of nature and everyday life, offering a vibrant insight into Roman art and interior decoration. The use of **marble** in floors, walls, and columns speaks to the opulence enjoyed by Ephesus's wealthy classes.

These houses also give a glimpse into the architecture of the period, with **advanced plumbing systems**, **well-designed rooms**, and **innovative heating** methods, providing a comprehensive look at daily life in ancient Ephesus.

Visiting the Terrace Houses is a must for those looking to understand the domestic life of Ephesus's upper class. It offers a fascinating contrast to the grand public spaces of the city, revealing how those who lived in the city's most **prestigious homes** experienced daily life.

Practical Tips:

- **Separate Entry**: Entrance to the Terrace Houses requires an additional ticket, so be sure to plan time for it.

- **Peak Hours**: Avoid the busiest times by visiting either early in the morning or in the late afternoon.

The Baths of Varius

The **Baths of Varius**, located near the **State Agora** in **Ephesus**, are a stunning example of Roman engineering and public leisure culture. These baths were built in the **1st century AD** and served as both a public bathing facility and a social hub for the citizens of Ephesus.

One of the most impressive features of the baths is the **hypocaust system**, a **heating method** that circulated warm air beneath the floors of the bathhouse to keep the rooms at a comfortable temperature. This innovation was one of many Roman advancements in architecture and engineering. The complex includes **changing rooms**, **marble floors**, and grand columns that demonstrate the luxurious nature of Roman bath culture.

The baths were not just for bathing; they were also a place to socialize, relax, and conduct business, offering a **communal** experience for people from all walks of life. The intricate stonework and the well-preserved structures reflect the bathhouse's importance in everyday Roman life, making it a remarkable part of the Ephesus archaeological site.

Practical Tips:

- **Finding the Baths**: The Baths of Varius are located near the **State Agora**, and are usually less crowded than the main attractions, making it an ideal spot to explore in peace.
- **Photography**: The **best time for photography** is in the morning when the light filters through the ruins, casting interesting shadows on the marble surfaces.

The Sacred Way

The **Sacred Way** in **Ephesus** was a ceremonial road that connected the **Temple of Artemis** to the city's urban center. This ancient path once played a central role in the city's religious festivals and processions, serving as the route for pilgrims making their way to one of the **Seven Wonders of the Ancient World**.

Walking along this **Sacred Way** allows visitors to connect with Ephesus's spiritual and civic past. Lined with **marble columns** and **statue bases**, the road once featured sculptures of gods, kings, and animals, reflecting the reverence the city had for its deities. Although much of the original grandeur of the road has been lost over time, parts of the marble paving and remnants of statues can still be seen, offering a powerful sense of the ancient path.

The **Sacred Way** was used for both **religious processions** and **festivals** held in honor of **Artemis**, the goddess of fertility and the hunt. Pilgrims would have walked this road as part of their journey to pay homage at the **Temple of Artemis**, one of the most important religious sites in the ancient world.

Practical Tips:

- **Walking Route**: The Sacred Way is a **peaceful spot** to walk, and it's ideal for visitors who want to enjoy a quieter, reflective experience in Ephesus.
- **Best Time to Visit**: The **early morning** or **late afternoon** offers the most tranquil atmosphere to walk this ancient path, with fewer crowds and cooler temperatures.

The Fountain of Polio

The **Fountain of Polio** is one of the lesser-known gems of **Ephesus**, yet it stands as a remarkable testament to the advanced **Roman engineering** and **urban planning**. Built in the **1st century AD** in honor of **Sextilius Pollio**, a wealthy benefactor, this **monumental water fountain** was a key source of water for the city.

The fountain is notable for its **intricate stonework**, **decorative reliefs**, and impressive **marble carvings** that tell the story of the Roman dedication to both **beauty** and **functionality**. The fountain once served not only as a public water source but also as a **decorative feature** in the **State Agora**, highlighting the importance of water management in Roman cities.

The Fountain of Pollio's **elegant design** and **reliefs** showcase the Roman love for combining **art** and **engineering**, making it one of the most visually striking and historically significant monuments in Ephesus. Visitors can appreciate the **skillful craftsmanship** of the marble reliefs and the functionality of the water system that once supplied the city.

Practical Tips:

- **Location**: The Fountain of Polio is located near the **State Agora** and can be accessed easily from the main path in Ephesus.
- **What to Look For**: Pay attention to the **intricate carvings** on the fountain, especially the **stone reliefs**, which depict important **Roman deities** and **symbols**.

The **Fountain of Pollio** serves as a reminder of the Romans' ability to create practical and **aesthetic public spaces**, symbolizing their mastery in both urban design and water engineering.

Outdoor Activities and Adventures

The region around **Ephesus** offers an incredible range of **outdoor activities** and **adventures**, blending the region's **rich history** with the **natural beauty** of the **Aegean coast**. Whether you're looking to explore ancient trails, relax on stunning beaches, or take in the area from the water, Ephesus and its surroundings have something for every type of adventurer.

For those interested in hiking, the paths leading from **Ephesus** to the **House of the Virgin Mary** or the **Ayasuluk Hill** near **Selçuk** provide both **scenic beauty** and **historical interest**. These hikes wind through **olive groves, rolling hills**, and offer breathtaking views of the surrounding countryside and coastline. Along the way, you can take in **ancient ruins** and quiet spots perfect for a reflective break.

If you're in the mood for water activities, nearby beaches such as **Pamucak Beach** and **Ladies Beach** in **Kusadasi** are ideal for sunbathing, swimming, and water sports. Many visitors enjoy activities like **jet skiing, parasailing**, and **beach volleyball**. Alternatively, explore the crystal-clear waters of the **Aegean Sea** through a boat tour, where you can take in hidden coves and swim in tranquil waters.

Practical Tips:

- **Best Times**: Spring and fall are the best times for outdoor activities in the region—when the weather is pleasant, and the summer crowds are thinner.
- **What to Bring**: Wear **comfortable footwear** for hiking and bring **sunscreen**, a **hat**, and plenty of **water**. For beach trips, pack swimwear, a towel, and a **camera** to capture the stunning scenery.

Hiking in the Ephesus Region

Hiking around **Ephesus** provides the perfect blend of **natural beauty** and **historical exploration**, making it a great option for travelers who enjoy both adventure and culture. The region offers a variety of scenic trails that wind through the countryside, offering not just beautiful vistas but also the chance to connect with the ancient world.

One of the most popular hiking routes starts at **Ephesus** and leads to the **House of the Virgin Mary**, a sacred pilgrimage site. This trail takes you through **rolling hills**, **olive groves**, and paths flanked by wildflowers, giving you a chance to immerse yourself in nature while exploring **historical landmarks** along the way. The journey is about **5 km** and can be completed in **1.5 to 2 hours** depending on your pace.

Another popular trail leads up to **Ayasuluk Hill**, located near **Selçuk**, which offers stunning views of the town, **Ephesus**, and the surrounding countryside. This relatively easy trail gives hikers a great chance to experience the natural beauty of the region while passing by ancient ruins like the **Selçuk Castle**.

Practical Tips:

- **Trail Difficulty**: These hikes are generally **moderate**, suitable for most travelers with **comfortable shoes**.
- **Duration**: Expect the hikes to take anywhere from **1.5 to 3 hours**, depending on your route and stops.
- **What to Bring**: Make sure to bring **plenty of water**, **comfortable hiking boots**, and **sun protection** as it can get hot during midday.

These trails provide a peaceful way to appreciate the stunning **Aegean landscape** while soaking up the ancient history of the region.

Exploring the Beaches near Ephesus

After a day of exploring the ruins of **Ephesus**, the nearby beaches offer the perfect opportunity to relax and unwind. The coastline near Ephesus is home to several **beautiful beaches**, known for their **soft sands**, **clear waters**, and scenic backdrops.

Pamucak Beach, located just **5 km** from **Ephesus**, is the most famous beach in the area. This **wide, sandy beach** is perfect for swimming, sunbathing, and enjoying the serene atmosphere. The beach is well-served with **cafés** and **restaurants**, where you can enjoy local seafood dishes while gazing at the clear blue sea.

If you're seeking a quieter spot, **Ladies Beach** in **Kusadasi** is another excellent option. While slightly more crowded, it offers **calm waters** and beautiful views. You can also enjoy a variety of **water sports** such as **jet skiing** and **parasailing**, or simply relax on the beach.

Practical Tips:

- **Getting There**: Pamucak Beach is easily accessible by taxi from **Selçuk**, or you can take a **local bus** from **Kusadasi**.
- **Best Time to Visit**: For fewer crowds, visit the beaches in **early morning** or **late afternoon**. Summer months can get very crowded, so **spring** and **fall** are ideal times to enjoy the coastline.

- **Activities**: Apart from swimming, you can try **snorkeling**, **jet skiing**, or **beach volleyball** on some of the more active beaches.

These beautiful beaches provide a relaxing escape after exploring the **ancient ruins** of Ephesus, offering plenty of opportunities to enjoy the natural beauty of Turkey's Aegean coast.

Boat Tours Along the Aegean Coast

For a unique perspective of the **Ephesus** region, take a **boat tour** along the **Aegean Coast**, departing from **Kusadasi**, just a short drive from the ancient site. Boat tours are a peaceful and scenic way to explore the coastline, offering a chance to swim in the **crystal-clear waters** and experience the beauty of hidden **coves** and **small islands**.

Half-day and **full-day boat trips** are available, with many including stops for **swimming** and **snorkeling**. Some tours even offer **traditional Turkish lunches** on board, allowing you to enjoy **local delicacies** while taking in the breathtaking views. You'll have the opportunity to explore **quiet beaches** that are only accessible by boat, far away from the crowds at the more popular beaches.

These boat trips also offer a chance to see **remote islands** and enjoy the tranquil beauty of the **Aegean Sea**. The **peaceful experience** of cruising along the coastline is a perfect complement to a busy day of sightseeing in Ephesus.

Practical Tips:

- **Booking**: You can book boat tours through **local tour operators** in **Kusadasi** or online. Prices generally range from **€25-60 per person**, depending on the tour duration and inclusions.
- **Best Time for Sailing**: The best time for boat tours is **spring** and **fall**, when the weather is mild and the seas are calm. During the summer, **booking in advance** is highly recommended due to high demand.
- **What to Bring**: Be sure to bring **swimwear**, **sunscreen**, and a **camera** to capture the stunning views and memorable experiences.

A boat tour along the **Aegean Coast** offers a peaceful, scenic retreat from the hustle and bustle of Ephesus and provides a unique way to experience the beauty of the region from the water.

Cultural Experiences

Ephesus and the surrounding region offer an enriching cultural experience where visitors can connect with the authenticity of **Turkish traditions** through **food**, **art**, and **local life**. In **Selçuk** and nearby towns, travelers can explore the heart of Turkish culture in vibrant **markets**, **festivals**, and **artisanal shops**.

A great way to immerse yourself in local culture is by visiting the bustling **Selçuk Market**, held weekly, where you can wander through rows of **handmade goods**, **spices**, and **fresh produce**. The market is an excellent place to sample **Turkish street food** like **simit** (a sesame-crusted bread) or **köfte** (grilled meatballs). The market also showcases traditional **handicrafts**, such as **woven textiles**, **carpets**, and **ceramics**, offering a perfect opportunity to engage with local artisans.

For an authentic taste of local cuisine, **cooking classes** are offered in **Selçuk**, where visitors can learn to make dishes like **gözleme** (stuffed flatbread) and **mezes** (small dishes served with bread). This hands-on experience is a delightful way to connect with the culture through food, while also enjoying the friendly hospitality of local hosts.

Additionally, **local performances** such as **Turkish folk dance** and **live music** offer a great chance to experience the artistic traditions of the region. These performances often take place during festivals or special events and are a wonderful way to see the cultural heritage come to life.

Practical Tips:

- Visit the **Selçuk Market** on **Saturdays** for fresh produce and local goods.
- Consider joining a **cooking class** to deepen your connection with Turkish food culture.

Immerse yourself in the warm, welcoming traditions of this region for a memorable and authentic experience.

Local Festivals and Events

Ephesus and the surrounding region host a variety of **local festivals** that bring Turkish culture to life in the most celebratory ways. These events showcase **art**, **music**, **dance**, and **traditional practices**, offering an opportunity to connect with the local community and experience the lively spirit of the region.

One of the most famous events is the **Selçuk Camel Wrestling Festival**, held every January. This **unique festival** involves camel wrestling, where beautifully adorned camels engage in a friendly competition, drawing both locals and visitors for a fun-filled day. The festival also features traditional **Turkish music, dance, and food stalls**, creating a vibrant atmosphere of community celebration.

Another notable festival is the **Ephesus Festival of Culture**, usually held in the summer, which celebrates the **arts** and **heritage** of the region. This festival includes **performances of classical music, theater**, and **dance**, often staged in historical venues like the **Great Theatre of Ephesus**. Visitors can enjoy spectacular performances in the ancient amphitheater while learning more about the region's **rich artistic history**.

For visitors looking for a taste of **local life**, regional festivals often feature **artisan markets**, where handmade goods such as **jewelry, pottery**, and **woven fabrics** are on display for sale.

Practical Tips:

- The **Selçuk Camel Wrestling Festival** takes place in **January**, while the **Ephesus Festival of Culture** occurs in **summer**.
- Check local event calendars for specific dates, as festivals may vary from year to year.

Attending one of these **local festivals** will not only give you a deeper appreciation for **Turkish traditions** but also provide an unforgettable cultural experience.

Turkish Cuisine: What to Try in Ephesus

Turkish cuisine is rich in flavors, with dishes that reflect the country's diverse history and cultural influences. In the **Ephesus region**, visitors are in for a culinary treat, with many local specialties waiting to be savored.

Kebabs are a must-try, with **Adana kebabs** (spicy minced meat) and **shish kebabs** (grilled skewers of marinated meat) being local favorites. Pair them with **mezes**, small dishes like **hummus, eggplant salad**, and **yogurt with herbs**, all perfect for sharing. Another regional specialty is **gözleme**, a savory Turkish flatbread filled with ingredients such as **cheese**, **spinach**, or **minced meat**.

For seafood lovers, **Ephesus** is just a short drive from the coast, meaning **fresh fish** and **grilled seafood** are abundant. **Turkish fish restaurants** in nearby **Kusadasi** offer everything from **grilled sea bass** to **fried calamari**. Pair these dishes with a glass of **rakı**, the Turkish aniseed liquor, for an authentic dining experience.

Desserts in Ephesus are unforgettable, particularly **baklava**, a sweet pastry layered with nuts and soaked in syrup. Don't forget to try **Turkish tea** or **coffee** after your meal, which is an essential part of Turkish hospitality.

Practical Tips:

- Enjoy **meze platters** with local bread at most restaurants in **Selçuk** and **Kusadasi**.
- **Lunch** is typically served from **12 PM to 3 PM**, so plan your day accordingly.

Ephesus offers a sensory feast for the taste buds, allowing visitors to savor both the **flavors** and **hospitality** of Turkish cuisine.

Traditional Crafts and Souvenirs

Ephesus is not only known for its **ancient ruins** but also for its vibrant **artisanal traditions**, where visitors can bring home a piece of **Turkish craftsmanship**. The region is home to a variety of **handmade goods**, from intricately woven **carpets** to **ceramic pots** and **decorative lamps**, each offering a unique reflection of Turkish culture.

Handwoven carpets are one of the most prized souvenirs. These **traditional Turkish rugs** feature intricate designs that reflect the country's long history of weaving and are made using techniques passed down through generations. Many shops in **Selçuk** and **Kusadasi** offer these **authentic** carpets, with an array of colors and patterns.

Ceramics are another highlight, with artisans producing beautiful **hand-painted tiles** and **vases**. These colorful, often geometric designs are a hallmark of Turkish artistry and make for stunning decor. For something more functional, **leather goods**, such as **handbags**, **jackets**, and **wallets**, are widely available and are known for their **durability** and **quality**.

The **grand bazaars** in **Selçuk** and **Kusadasi** are the perfect places to find these crafts. While shopping, it's essential to know how to **bargain** respectfully—this is part of the culture, and sellers expect some negotiation.

Practical Tips:

- **Authenticity**: Look for **artisan cooperatives** or **local workshops** to ensure the crafts are handmade.
- **Bargaining**: Start by offering **half** the asking price, then negotiate to find a fair deal.

Purchasing **local crafts** not only supports the region's economy but also helps preserve **traditional skills** that have been practiced for centuries. It's a great way to

Dining and Nightlife

After a day of exploring the **ancient ruins of Ephesus**, visitors can unwind and savor the region's **rich culinary traditions** in Selçuk and **Kusadasi**, two nearby towns that offer an exciting mix of **traditional dining** and laid-back nightlife.

Start your evening with a **Turkish meal** at one of the many **local restaurants** that specialize in **fresh, flavorful** dishes. **Meze platters**, filled with small, delicious bites like **hummus, eggplant salad**, and **dolma** (stuffed grape leaves), are perfect for sharing and sampling a variety of flavors. For a heartier meal, try **kebabs, lamb chops**, or **fish dishes**, all made using the freshest **local ingredients**. **Seafood**, in particular, is a highlight in **Kusadasi**, known for its coastal location.

As night falls, the **vibrant nightlife** scene comes alive, especially in **Kusadasi**, where you'll find a range of **beach bars, rooftop lounges**, and **cozy wine bars**. Enjoy a relaxing evening with a glass of **raki** (the Turkish aniseed drink) while listening to **live music** or traditional **Turkish folk performances**. In **Selçuk**, the atmosphere is more laid-back, with **local taverns** and small bars offering a chance to unwind with a drink and **good conversation**.

Practical Tips:

- **Best Dining Times**: **Dinner** is typically served from **7 PM to 10 PM**.
- **Nightlife Hours**: Bars and lounges are generally open from **8 PM until midnight**, with later hours in **Kusadasi**.
- **Vegetarian Options**: Many places offer **vegetarian-friendly** options, especially in **meze platters**.

Whether you're looking to **relax** over dinner or enjoy a **night out**, the region offers plenty of opportunities to indulge in **authentic Turkish cuisine** and experience its **vibrant nighttime culture**.

Best Restaurants in Ephesus

Around **Ephesus**, the nearby town of **Selçuk** and **Kusadasi** offer a wide range of **authentic Turkish restaurants**, from family-run taverns to sophisticated seafood eateries. Here are some top-rated spots to try:

- **Selçuk Koftecisi**: Known for its **delicious meatballs (köfte)**, this small, family-run restaurant in Selçuk offers a cozy atmosphere and excellent service. The meatballs are served with a side of **fresh bread** and **yogurt**, making for a satisfying meal.

- **Ejder Restaurant**: Located in **Selçuk**, Ejder is famous for its **traditional Turkish dishes**, including **lamb kebabs** and **mezes**. The **outdoor seating** is perfect for a meal while soaking up the relaxed village ambiance.

- **Kuşadası Seafood Restaurants**: Kusadasi, being a coastal town, is the place to go for **fresh seafood**. Restaurants like **Koru Seafood** offer a stunning view of the **Aegean Sea** while serving **grilled fish**, **seafood stews**, and **traditional Turkish appetizers**.

These restaurants provide a range of experiences, from **casual** and **budget-friendly** to **elegant fine dining**.

Practical Tips:

- **Vegetarian Options**: Most restaurants offer vegetarian dishes, with meze being a popular choice.
- **Reservation**: For popular spots like **Ejder Restaurant** or the seaside eateries in Kusadasi, it's best to **reserve in advance** during high season.
- **Signature Dishes**: Don't miss the **Aegean seafood, grilled lamb**, and **baklava** for dessert.

These local gems offer a wonderful blend of **traditional flavors**, **warm hospitality**, and a true taste of the **Ephesus region**.

Traditional Turkish Dining Experiences

When in the **Ephesus region**, don't miss the opportunity to experience **traditional Turkish dining** at local **lokantas** and **family-run restaurants**, where meals are more than just food—they are an experience.

In Turkey, food plays a central role in culture, and meals are often a social event. At a **lokanta**, you'll find simple, home-style dishes like **lentil soup (mercimek çorbası)**, **stuffed vine leaves (dolma)**, and **lamb kebabs**. The **meze** platter, filled with an assortment of small appetizers, is commonly shared among friends or family, reflecting the communal nature of Turkish dining.

Another must-try is **gözleme**, a type of **Turkish flatbread** stuffed with ingredients like **spinach**, **cheese**, or **minced meat**, cooked fresh and served warm. The joy of eating in Turkey is often tied to the **atmosphere**—many restaurants feature **outdoor terraces**, where you can dine under **olive trees** or in **village settings**, making your meal even more delightful.

Practical Tips:

- **How to Order**: It's common to **order meze platters** to share, followed by a **main dish** like kebabs or stews. Don't forget to ask for **Turkish tea** or **coffee** after the meal!
- **Tipping Etiquette**: **Tipping** in Turkey is customary, generally around **10-15%** of the bill. It's a way to show appreciation for the meal and service.

Dining in the Ephesus region is a cultural journey in itself, where food isn't just about flavor but about experiencing the **generosity and warmth** of Turkish hospitality.

Bars and Nightclubs in the Region

The nightlife scene around **Ephesus** is laid-back yet vibrant, offering a variety of **bars** and **nightclubs** in nearby **Kusadasi** and **Selçuk** where visitors can unwind after a day of exploring the ruins. Kusadasi, being a popular **coastal resort town**, has a more lively nightlife, while Selçuk offers a **quieter** and **more relaxed** atmosphere.

In **Kusadasi**, you'll find several **beach bars** along the coastline, where you can sip cocktails while watching the sunset over the **Aegean Sea. Kusadasi's Marina**, lined with **rooftop lounges** and **live music bars**, provides a chic spot to enjoy a **night out**. **The British Corner Pub** offers a **cosmopolitan vibe** with a mix of **local beer**, cocktails, and **live performances**.

For those looking for a more **traditional** experience, **Selçuk** offers several cozy **wine bars** and **local taverns** where **Turkish folk music** fills the air. **Café Sirince**, just outside **Selçuk**, is a great place to enjoy **traditional Turkish music** while sipping on a **glass of wine** made from local vineyards.

Practical Tips:

- **Popular Venues**: In **Kusadasi**, visit **The Marina** area for vibrant nightlife, or head to **Selçuk** for a more relaxed evening.
- **Opening Hours**: Most bars in **Kusadasi** stay open until **late** at night, whereas in **Selçuk**, nightlife usually winds down earlier, around **midnight**.
- **Drink Prices**: Expect to pay around **€4-8** for drinks in **Kusadasi** bars, with prices being a bit lower in **Selçuk**.

Whether you're after a **night of dancing** or a **quiet evening with a drink**, Ephesus's surrounding towns offer something for every type of traveler.

Shopping in Ephesus

Shopping in and around **Ephesus** is not just about buying souvenirs; it's an opportunity to immerse yourself in the **rich cultural heritage** of the region. Visitors will find **traditional markets** filled with **artisan goods**, **handcrafted treasures**, and **locally made products** that reflect Turkey's deep craftsmanship traditions. Whether wandering through the vibrant **Selçuk Market** or browsing small boutiques in **Kusadasi**, you're sure to discover authentic items that connect you with local culture.

In **Selçuk**, you'll find a charming **bazaar-style market** where **handmade jewelry, embroidered textiles**, and **pottery** are sold by passionate local artisans. The friendly **shopkeepers** are eager to share their stories, making the shopping experience not just about purchasing, but about **connecting with local traditions**. You can also find **spices** and **herbs** used in Turkish cuisine, adding a fragrant touch to your souvenirs.

For an extra special touch, visit the **artisan cooperatives** in nearby villages, where local craftsmen still create their pieces the old-fashioned way, such as **weaving carpets** or **painting ceramics**. Watching the process firsthand allows you to appreciate the **skill** and **heritage** behind these beautiful items.

Practical Tips:

- Always ask about the **craftsmanship** to ensure the authenticity of your purchase.
- Don't forget to **bargain**—it's part of the fun and tradition in Turkish markets.

Shopping here is an opportunity to take home more than just items; you're bringing back a piece of **Ephesus's culture**.

Souvenir Shopping: What to Buy

When visiting **Ephesus**, you'll find an array of **souvenirs** that capture the essence of Turkish craftsmanship and culture. From **handmade jewelry** to **traditional Turkish textiles**, there's no shortage of meaningful keepsakes to bring home.

One of the most iconic souvenirs is the **evil eye charm (Nazar Boncuğu)**, a symbol of **protection** and **good luck** in Turkish culture. You can find these charms in all shapes and sizes, from keychains to decorative pieces, at **Selçuk Market** or near the **Ephesus ruins**.

If you're looking for something more personal, consider purchasing **handmade jewelry** featuring local **silver** and **gemstones**. These intricate pieces often tell stories of the region's **history** and **tradition**. Additionally, **Turkish**

delight (lokum) is a delicious and memorable souvenir. The sweet, chewy confection is made in various flavors like rose, pistachio, and lemon and is perfect for sharing with friends and family back home.

For wine lovers, **local wines** from the Ephesus region are also great souvenirs to take home.

Practical Tips:

- Check the **craftsmanship** to ensure you're buying authentic **handmade** products, not mass-produced items.
- **Bargaining** is common in markets—start by offering half the asking price and work from there.

With these tips, you can ensure your souvenirs are both authentic and meaningful.

Local Markets and Bazaar Guide

The **local markets** and **bazaars** around **Ephesus** are some of the most vibrant and immersive parts of the region, offering travelers a chance to explore local life and culture through the art of shopping. **Selçuk Market**, held every **Saturday**, is a must-visit, with its mix of fresh **produce**, **spices**, **handmade textiles**, and **crafts**. The market is filled with the scent of **herbs**, the buzz of conversation, and the sight of colorful **fruit and vegetables** stacked high on vendor stalls. Here, you can enjoy **friendly banter** with local vendors as you browse their goods, making for a **personalized shopping experience**.

For those seeking a larger and more bustling market, **Kusadasi** offers a lively shopping scene with larger **bazaar areas**. Here, you can shop for **clothing**, **jewelry**, and **handicrafts** while soaking in the **colorful atmosphere**. Don't miss the **Tire Market**, held on Saturdays in the nearby town of Tire, which is famous for its **handwoven carpets** and local products.

Practical Tips:

- **Best Visiting Hours**: Early morning is the best time to visit, avoiding the crowds and enjoying cooler temperatures.
- **Bargaining**: Always be prepared to haggle. It's part of the tradition, and a fun way to engage with the locals.

The lively markets of the Ephesus region provide a unique shopping experience, where you can find not just products, but a **taste of local culture** and **hospitality**.

Where to Find Authentic Turkish Textiles and Ceramics

Ephesus and the surrounding areas are famous for their high-quality, **handcrafted textiles** and **ceramics**. The region is home to **skilled artisans** who create **unique, beautiful products** that reflect centuries of tradition and craftsmanship.

Turkish carpets and **kilims** are the ultimate souvenir from the region. These **woven treasures**, often made from **wool** or **silk**, feature traditional **patterns** and **symbols** passed down through generations. You can find authentic carpets in **Selçuk**, particularly in **artisan cooperatives** where local weavers produce **handmade** rugs and **textiles**.

Similarly, **ceramics** from the Ephesus region are renowned for their intricate designs and vibrant colors. **Hand-painted pottery**, including **plates**, **bowls**, and **vases**, often feature **floral motifs** and **traditional symbols**. Visit **local workshops** to see artisans at work and purchase these **authentic** pieces directly from the creators.

When buying **Turkish carpets** or **ceramics**, it's important to understand the difference between **mass-produced** items and those made by **local artisans**.

Genuine pieces will carry the mark of craftsmanship, such as slight imperfections that reflect the hand-made process.

Practical Tips:

- **Look for Authenticity**: Ask the artisan about the **production process** and the **materials** used.
- **Price Range**: Turkish carpets and ceramics can be expensive, but you can find more affordable options for smaller items like **ceramic tiles** or **small vases**.
- **Bargaining**: Don't hesitate to **negotiate** prices, especially in **markets**.

By purchasing **authentic Turkish textiles and ceramics**, you support **local artisans** while taking home a piece of **Ephesus's rich cultural heritage**.

Day Trips from Ephesus

Ephesus is surrounded by a wealth of exciting destinations, perfect for day trips that complement your visit to the ancient city. Whether you're drawn to **natural wonders**, charming **villages**, or additional **cultural sites**, there's something for every traveler just a short distance from **Selçuk** or **Kusadasi**.

One of the most popular day trips is to **Pamukkale**, a UNESCO World Heritage site famous for its stunning **white travertine terraces** filled with warm, mineral-rich water. A three-hour drive from **Selçuk**, Pamukkale offers a unique opportunity to **bathe** in the terraces and explore the nearby **Hierapolis** ruins.

For a quieter, more traditional experience, head to **Şirince Village**, a picturesque hilltop village just 8 kilometers from **Selçuk**. Known for its cobblestone streets, **historic houses**, and **local wines**, it's an excellent place to sample Turkish wines and explore the **countryside**.

Additionally, a visit to the **Aegean coast** for a **boat tour** or a stop at nearby **Kusadasi** for its bustling **markets** and beautiful **beaches** makes for a relaxing alternative. The combination of **ancient ruins** and **modern charm** will surely extend the allure of your Ephesus adventure.

Practical Tips:

- **Transportation**: You can easily reach these destinations via **local buses**, **private tours**, or **renting a car**.
- **Travel Time**: Most destinations are within a **1-3 hour drive** from **Selçuk**.

Embark on a journey that blends the past and present, offering new experiences that will enrich your time in the Ephesus region.

Pamukkale and the Thermal Pools

Pamukkale, meaning "Cotton Castle" in Turkish, is one of the country's most awe-inspiring natural wonders and a must-visit day trip from **Ephesus**. Known for its stunning **white travertine terraces**, Pamukkale is formed by **thermal waters** that cascade down the mountainside, creating pools of warm, mineral-rich water. The terraces appear as though they are covered in white snow, but they are actually deposits of **calcium carbonate** formed over thousands of years.

In addition to the **thermal pools**, visitors can explore the **ancient city of Hierapolis**, located just above Pamukkale. The ruins of **temples**, **baths**, and an **ancient theater** offer a fascinating glimpse into the history of this once-thriving Roman city. Visitors can even relax in the **ancient pool** where warm waters flow over Roman columns submerged beneath the water's surface.

Practical Tips:

- **Distance**: Pamukkale is about a **3-hour drive** from **Ephesus** or **Selçuk**. You can book a **guided tour, private transfer**, or drive on your own.
- **Best Time to Visit**: Early morning or late afternoon to avoid the midday heat and crowds.
- **Entrance Fees**: There is a small **entrance fee** for both the **thermal pools** and the **Hierapolis ruins**.
- **What to Bring**: Swimwear, water shoes, sunscreen, and a camera to capture the stunning landscapes.

Pamukkale's beauty and serenity make it a perfect escape, where nature and history merge into a breathtaking experience.

Şirince Village: A Taste of Traditional Turkey

Just a short drive from **Ephesus**, the **charming village of Şirince** is a delightful destination that offers a taste of traditional Turkish life. This hillside village is known for its **cobblestone streets**, **historic stone houses**, and breathtaking views of the surrounding **mountains** and

olive groves. The village's **village charm** is heightened by its quaint atmosphere, where locals maintain ancient traditions.

Şirince is also renowned for its **local wine-making**—visit the **family-owned vineyards** and sample wines made from fruit like **figs, apricots**, and **peaches**. The village is a great place to enjoy a leisurely meal with traditional dishes like **Turkish breakfast** (served with olives, cheese, honey, and fresh bread) or **gözleme** (stuffed flatbread).

Besides food and drink, Şirince offers wonderful shopping opportunities. Explore **artisan stalls** selling **handmade** goods, such as **olive oil soaps, embroidered textiles**, and **ceramics**.

Practical Tips:

- **How to Reach**: Şirince is just a **15-minute drive** from **Selçuk**. You can also take a **minibus** from **Selçuk** for a more affordable option.
- **Best Time to Visit**: Spring or autumn when the weather is pleasant and the village is less crowded.
- **Exploring**: Wander through the narrow streets, and don't forget to stop by the **local wineries** for a tasting session.

A visit to Şirince offers an intimate look into Turkey's rural life, providing a perfect complement to the ancient ruins of Ephesus.

Selçuk: Exploring the Surrounding Area

Selçuk, the small town located just outside **Ephesus**, offers an abundance of historical and cultural experiences that make it an ideal base for exploring the region. The town itself is rich in history, home to attractions such as the **Basilica of St. John**, where the apostle is believed to be buried, and the **Ayasuluk Fortress**, offering panoramic views of the surrounding countryside.

The **Isa Bey Mosque** is another must-see in Selçuk. Built in the **14th century**, it is considered one of the most beautiful examples of **Seljuk architecture** in Anatolia. The mosque's **intricate tilework** and stunning **courtyard** make it a peaceful retreat from the bustling town.

Selçuk also has a **weekly market**, which is the perfect place to pick up **local produce**, **handmade crafts**, and **spices**. For a deeper dive into the ancient city's history, don't miss the **Ephesus Archaeological Museum**, which houses important artifacts from the ruins of

Ephesus, including **statues of Artemis**, **coins**, and mosaics.

Practical Tips:

- **How to Spend the Day**: After touring **Ephesus**, visit the **Basilica of St. John**, explore the **Ayasuluk Fortress**, and wander through the **local market**.
- **Dining**: Enjoy a meal at one of the **local taverns** or **family-run restaurants** serving traditional Turkish dishes.
- **Transport**: **Selçuk** is easily accessible on foot from **Ephesus** or by **local taxis**.

Selçuk offers a wonderful blend of **history** and **local culture**, making it the perfect destination for visitors who want to explore more of the Ephesus region.

Travel Tips for Ephesus

Visiting **Ephesus** is an unforgettable experience, and with a little preparation, your trip can be smooth and enjoyable. Here are some essential **travel tips** to help you make the most of your time in this ancient city.

Firstly, **communication** in Ephesus is generally easy for tourists. While **Turkish** is the official language, **English** is widely spoken in popular areas like **Selçuk** and **Kusadasi**. It's always appreciated when travelers make the effort to learn a few basic phrases like **"Merhaba"** (Hello) or **"Teşekkür ederim"** (Thank you), though locals are happy to help with English if needed.

When it comes to **money**, the official currency is the **Turkish Lira (TRY)**. Most **hotels**, **restaurants**, and **shops** accept **credit cards**, but it's a good idea to carry **cash** for smaller establishments or markets. You can easily withdraw cash from **ATMs** or exchange your money at **currency exchange offices** in **Selçuk** or **Kusadasi**. Remember to carry small denominations for convenience, especially for **tipping** or paying for **small purchases**.

Safety is generally not a concern in **Ephesus**—the area is considered **very safe** for tourists. However, it's always wise to keep an eye on your belongings, especially in busy areas. In the summer, the sun can be intense, so wear **sunscreen** and **stay hydrated** while exploring the ruins. **Pharmacies** and **medical services** are available in **Selçuk** in case of emergencies.

Lastly, be sure to carry **travel insurance** for peace of mind. With a few simple precautions, your trip to **Ephesus** will be both enjoyable and safe.

Language and Communication Tips

While the official language of **Ephesus** is **Turkish**, you'll find that **English** is widely spoken, especially in tourist-friendly areas like **Selçuk** and **Kusadasi**. However, learning a few key **Turkish phrases** can go a long way in making a positive connection with locals and showing respect for their culture.

Start with some simple greetings:

- **Merhaba** (Hello)
- **Günaydın** (Good morning)
- **Teşekkür ederim** (Thank you)
- **Lütfen** (Please)

If you're trying to ask how someone is doing, use:

- **Nasılsınız?** (How are you?) (formal)
- **Nasılsın?** (How are you?) (informal)

In most tourist destinations, **English** is sufficient, but when shopping in **markets** or dealing with **taxi drivers**, knowing a few words will make interactions more pleasant and authentic.

For situations where communication is difficult, don't hesitate to use **translation apps** like **Google Translate**. Many shopkeepers, waiters, and hotel staff are accustomed to using these apps to help travelers.

When you're at a restaurant or shop, be aware of **non-verbal cues**, as hand gestures are also a helpful communication tool. If unsure, always smile and ask for help. Turkish people are known for their **hospitality** and will appreciate your effort to communicate in their native language.

Currency and Payment Methods

When visiting **Ephesus**, the official currency is the **Turkish Lira (TRY)**. While **credit cards** are accepted in most **hotels**, **restaurants**, and larger **tourist shops**, you'll still want to carry **cash** for smaller markets, street vendors, and more traditional eateries.

ATMs are widely available in **Selçuk** and **Kusadasi**, so withdrawing cash is easy. Be aware that some ATMs may charge a small fee for international withdrawals, so it's best to choose ATMs located near banks. Currency exchange offices are also found in **Selçuk** and **Kusadasi**, offering competitive exchange rates.

When it comes to **tipping**, **10-15%** is customary in restaurants, though tipping is **not mandatory**. In more casual settings, leaving **small change** is appreciated. In markets, **bargaining** is part of the experience, and sellers will often expect you to negotiate prices.

For practical use, it's advisable to carry **small denominations** (try to get bills in 5, 10, or 20 Lira) to make purchases and tips easier. Turkish currency is straightforward, with bills in denominations of **5, 10, 20, 50, 100**, and **200 Lira**.

Safety and Health Tips

Ephesus is a **safe destination** for tourists, but like any popular tourist location, it's always a good idea to take some **basic precautions** to ensure your safety and well-being.

Health-wise, it's crucial to stay **hydrated** during the summer months, especially when exploring the ruins of Ephesus, where the sun can be quite intense. Carry a **water bottle** and **sunscreen**, and wear a **hat** to protect yourself from the sun. Comfortable shoes are essential for walking on the ancient pathways, which can be **uneven** in places.

In case of illness or injury, there are **pharmacies** and **medical centers** available in **Selçuk** and **Kusadasi**, both of which cater to **tourists** and **locals alike**. For **minor ailments** like headaches or stomach issues, these pharmacies are an excellent resource.

Although **Ephesus** is a very **safe** area, be aware of your surroundings in **crowded places** like markets and tourist spots. **Pickpocketing** is a possibility, so keep your **valuables** close and in a **secure bag**. When using **taxis** or **public transport**, always check for official **licenses** and agree on fares in advance.

Lastly, consider purchasing **travel insurance** to ensure you're covered in case of unforeseen emergencies. With these simple tips, you can enjoy your time in Ephesus with peace of mind.

Local Etiquette and Customs

Understanding **local etiquette** in **Ephesus** is key to showing respect for Turkish culture. Turkey is known for its **warm hospitality**, and by following a few simple customs, you'll blend in effortlessly and make a positive impression.

Start with the basics: greeting people with a **friendly** **"Merhaba"** (Hello) is always appreciated. **Politeness** is important, especially when interacting with older people or in formal settings. **"Teşekkür ederim"** (Thank you) is an essential phrase that reflects your appreciation for their service or help.

When visiting **religious sites** such as **mosques**, it's customary to wear **modest clothing**, covering your shoulders and knees. Women may be required to wear a **headscarf**, which is often provided at the entrance. At **holy sites** or **shrines**, always **show respect**—keep noise levels down and avoid inappropriate gestures.

When dining, **sharing meals** is a significant part of Turkish hospitality. Meals are often served family-style, with multiple dishes for everyone to enjoy. If offered **Turkish tea** or **coffee**, accept graciously, as it's part of the local culture. In restaurants, tipping **10-15%** is customary, and in smaller shops or eateries, leaving **small change** is appreciated.

Lastly, when shopping in **markets**, it's **polite to bargain**, but always do so with a **smile** and in a respectful manner. Bargaining is seen as a fun part of the shopping experience, and shopkeepers will often engage in friendly conversation.

By understanding these simple **customs**, you'll ensure a warm and respectful experience while visiting **Ephesus** and the surrounding area.

Practical Information

Visiting **Ephesus** is a memorable experience, and having the right practical information can make your trip smoother. Here are some essential details to help you plan:

Opening Hours: Most attractions, including the **Ancient City of Ephesus** and **Ephesus Archaeological Museum**, are open daily. They typically open at **8:00 AM** and close around **7:00 PM** during peak summer months, with slightly shorter hours during the winter. The **House of the Virgin Mary** and **Temple of Artemis** generally operate from **8:00 AM to 5:00 PM**. Always check the schedules, as **early closures** might occur during national holidays or religious festivals.

Entrance Fees: Entrance to the **Ephesus Archaeological Site** costs around **100 TRY**. Additional sites, like the **Terrace Houses**, have a separate fee of **30 TRY**. The **Ephesus Museum** charges approximately **20 TRY**, while the **House of the Virgin Mary** costs about **40 TRY**. Consider purchasing a **combined ticket** for a discount on multiple sites. Some sites offer **audio guides** or **guided tours** for an extra fee, generally ranging from **50-100 TRY**.

Payment Methods: Credit and debit cards are accepted at most ticket counters, though it's a good idea to carry **cash** for smaller purchases, like parking or local souvenirs.

Transportation: **Buses** are available from **Selçuk** to most major sites. Taxis are also common, but be sure to agree on the fare in advance.

With this practical info, you'll be ready for an efficient and enjoyable visit to **Ephesus**.

Opening Hours of Major Attractions

The major **attractions in Ephesus** generally follow consistent opening hours, but it's important to know the seasonal variations for an optimal visit.

- **Ancient City of Ephesus**: Open from **8:00 AM** to **7:00 PM** (summer). In winter, it may close earlier, typically by **5:00 PM**.
- **Ephesus Archaeological Museum**: Open daily from **8:30 AM** to **5:30 PM** (closed on Mondays). Hours may be reduced during the off-season.
- **House of the Virgin Mary**: Open **8:00 AM - 5:00 PM** daily, with extended hours in summer.
- **Temple of Artemis**: Access is free, as only ruins remain, but the site is available to visit at any time during daylight hours.

For the best experience, it's recommended to arrive **early in the morning** or later in the **afternoon** to avoid peak crowds, especially during the summer. Visiting in **spring** or **fall** provides pleasant temperatures and fewer tourists.

Do note that during **religious or national holidays**, these sites might close earlier or have limited access, so check the schedule in advance.

Entrance Fees

When visiting **Ephesus**, here's a breakdown of the **entrance fees** for the top attractions:

- **Ephesus Archaeological Site**: Entrance fee is approximately **100 TRY**.
- **Terrace Houses**: These require a separate ticket priced at **30 TRY**.
- **Ephesus Museum**: **20 TRY** for general entry.
- **House of the Virgin Mary**: Entry costs **40 TRY**.

Consider purchasing **combined tickets**, which allow access to multiple sites (like **Ephesus Archaeological Site, Terrace Houses,** and **Ephesus Museum**) at a discounted rate. Prices for combined tickets range from **150-180 TRY**.

You can buy tickets at the **on-site counters**, or some attractions may offer **online ticketing** options for convenience and to avoid long queues. **Audio guides** or **guided tours** are available at most sites, with prices typically ranging from **50-100 TRY** depending on the service.

Most places accept **credit/debit cards**, but it's always good to have **cash** on hand for smaller purchases, like souvenirs or tips.

Useful Local Contact Information

When traveling to **Ephesus**, it's helpful to know key local contact information for emergencies, transportation, and services:

Emergency Numbers:

- **Police**: 155
- **Ambulance**: 112
- **Fire**: 110

Tourist Information:

- **Selçuk Tourist Information Office**: Located in the town center. They provide maps, local event details, and advice on attractions.

Transportation:

- **Taxi Services**: Available throughout **Selçuk** and **Kusadasi**. Ensure you agree on the fare before starting the ride.
- **Bus Station**: The **Selçuk Bus Station** offers connections to **Kusadasi**, **Izmir**, and other regional towns.

Pharmacies and Medical Services:

- **Selçuk State Hospital**: Located in Selçuk for general medical needs.
- **Pharmacies**: Available in **Selçuk** for over-the-counter medicines and other essentials.

If you're an international traveler, don't forget to have the **contact information for your embassy** in case of emergencies.

By keeping these numbers and resources handy, you'll be prepared for any unexpected situations during your visit to **Ephesus**.

Conclusion

Ephesus is more than just an ancient city—it's a **living testament** to the triumphs of human history, a place where the past **whispers through every stone** and where the present is infused with the spirit of the people who have called this region home for centuries. Stepping into the ruins of **Ephesus** is like stepping back in time, where you can walk the same marble streets that once bustled with merchants, scholars, and worshippers, or marvel at the grandeur of the **Library of Celsus** and the **Great Theatre**, which have withstood the test of time.

But Ephesus is not only about its archaeological wonders—it's about the **warmth** of the Turkish people, the vibrant **culture**, and the stunning **Aegean landscape** that surrounds it. Whether you're wandering the ancient streets, tasting local delicacies, or sipping tea with a friendly local artisan, Ephesus offers a rich blend of history, nature, and hospitality.

Visiting Ephesus is a journey that transcends time. It's an opportunity to **connect with the past** while enjoying the comforts and charm of modern Turkey. The memories you create here—the awe of standing before the **Temple of Artemis**, the serenity of the **House of the Virgin Mary**, or the joy of shopping in **Selçuk's bustling markets**—will stay with you long after you leave.

If you haven't already, make **Ephesus** a priority on your travel bucket list. Let it inspire you, move you, and remind you of the incredible depth and beauty that our world holds. It's a destination that promises not just a trip, but a **journey of the soul**. Plan your visit today and let the magic of Ephesus unfold before you.

Printed in Dunstable, United Kingdom